"An inspiring reflection that reinforces the power of the human spirit, relationships, and love. A fresh perspective that reminds us why a diagnosis of cancer can open our eyes and bring us the opportunity to gain new heights in life."

—Richard Curry, MD
Neuro-Oncologist, physician to Donna

"By believing in God, Donna overcame the worst prognostic disease, teaching us the power of belief and, I believe, stimulating an immune response to the tumor. It is people like Donna, with an unpredictable situation, telling us that it is absolutely not over yet. Keep up your deep and true belief in God. Everything that happens fits into a pattern for good, to those who love God."

—Set Shahbabian, MD
Neurological Surgeon, physician to Donna

"Donna witnessed to her entire medical team by her faith and courage. Larry, too, witnessed to us by his unwavering support for his bride— in sickness and in health. This is a powerful story for those seeking hope and encouragement."

—Thaddeus M. Bort, MD
Cincinnati, OH

"Here at Crossroads Church, we deeply believe that our growth in God is achieved, in part, by our transparency with one another: faults, strengths, and everything in between. Larry's willingness to share his and Donna's story has—and continues to—benefit our community. Larry is a man open to God, and trusting the path through the unknown to get more of Him."

—Scott Dill
Director of Spiritual Support, Crossroads Church

"While this is a book that Larry would not have written if his wife had not been diagnosed with a terminal cancer, in my mind, the scope can be a positive resource to anyone seeking—or needing—resiliency. I recommend it as a source of encouragement, guidance and blessing to those whose lives have been thrown more than a curveball—be it cancer or otherwise."

—**Dwight Young**
Director, BLOC Ministries and longtime friend of Larry and Donna

"Courageous: A word that describes the physical and spiritual journey of Larry and Donna for the past five years. From day one of Donna's illness, Larry has been the embodiment of hope. He had the courage to say openly, 'Donna will beat the odds.' Yet, even though their life experience was teaching them that God is trustworthy, Larry allowed darkness into his soul. The result was a crisis of faith; hope and courage came with a high price. The renewing of his faith came in the middle of the storm, as he recognized just how good and trustworthy God is. This realization of God's goodness brought Larry to repentance. This repentance included a willingness to establish relationships with other men and to comfort and encourage them, as he had been encouraged and comforted by the Lord. I have had the privilege of being a witness to two miracles. The first, the healing of Donna's body and the longevity of her life. The second, the healing of Larry's soul. It is, indeed, an honor to be a part of their lives and to call them MY FRIENDS. Read—and be blessed!"

—**Rick Iles**
Longtime friend of Larry and Donna

STAYING RESILIENT

When Life Throws You More Than a Curveball

STAYING RESILIENT

When Life Throws You More Than a Curveball

Lawrence R. Blundred

WINTERS
PUBLISHING

winterspublishing.com

Winters Publishing
P.O. Box 501
Greensburg, Indiana 47240

Staying Resilient When Life Throws You More Than A Curveball

Printed in: United States of America
Project editors: Marjorie Redford, Karen Cain, and Joann Van Meter
Cover design: Dale Meyers
Interior design: Tracy Winters

Photo credits:
Lighthouse on page 13: iStock.com/NikonShutterman
Baseball on pages 19, 27, 35, 43, 53, 67, 79, and 87 © Tage Olsin / Wikipedia Commons / CC-SA
Dog on page 55: phili19/Shutterstock.com
All other photos provided by author.

The author has added italics and bold typeface to some Scripture quotations for emphasis.

Any Internet addresses (websites, blogs, etc.) in this book are offered as a resource. They are not intended in any way to be or imply an endorsement by the Publisher, nor does the Publisher vouch for the content of these sites for the life of this book.

Published by Winters Publishing
www.winterspublishing.com

ISBN: 978-1-883651-85-5

Library of Congress Control Number: 2017910413

22 21 20 19 18 17   1 2 3 4 5 6 7 8 9

DEDICATION

I dedicate this writing to my wife, Donna, "The Thriver," who has inspired so many others and me. And to the Brave Journey at Crossroads Church, where the vision first unfolded. And last, but not least, to so many men and women inside and outside of our Brave Journey and cancer support groups who have challenged, encouraged, and mentored me in this journey of healing and restoration. You have been my "lighthouses."

If any financial gain-profit is realized from this project, I will tithe, at minimum, 30% of these gains-profits equally to benefit the UC Brain Tumor Center at the University of Cincinnati Gardner Neuroscience Institute, Crossroads Church, and BLOC (Believing Living One Christ) Ministries. Believing Living One Christ BLOC

"It ain't over till it's over."[1]
—Yogi Berra

CONTENTS

FOREWORD

A brain tumor is an "abnormal growth of tissue in the brain or central spine that can disrupt proper brain function."[1] Primary brain tumors begin in the brain and tend to stay in the brain, whereas metastatic brain tumors begin as a cancer elsewhere in the body and spread to the brain.

According to the American Brain Tumor Association, brain tumors "do not discriminate." Primary brain tumors are statistically more frequent in children and older adults, but they can affect people of any age. One report (updated in January 2017 by the ABTA) states that nearly 700,000 people in the US are living with primary brain and central nervous system tumors. The same report predicts that nearly 17,000 people will lose their battles against brain tumors in 2017.[2]

Treatment for brain tumors varies. Most patients work with a team of specialists that includes a neurologist, oncologist, surgeon, pathologist, social worker, nutritionist, and more. But what team provides treatment and care for the patient's spouse or caregiver? A social worker might offer advice on changes in daily routines that the spouse should expect. A pastor or chaplain might stop by and voice a prayer. Friends may call to say, "Let us know what we can do for you." (They may even bring over a few meals.) But until you go through the situation yourself, there is no way to truly understand what "treatment" will be most effective for the health and healing of the person walking alongside the spouse, friend, or loved one who has been diagnosed with a brain tumor or any other diagnosis that has left "It's over" or "We are sorry" ringing in your ears.

Larry Blundred, author of this book, is and has been there. When his wife Donna was diagnosed in June 2012 with a Grade IV glioblastoma multiforme (GMB) brain tumor, everything in his life—and theirs—changed. In *Staying Resilient*, Larry candidly reveals the journey he has taken alongside Donna. As Larry tells his story, he tells what has helped him to rise above anger and bitterness. He openly shares his faith and belief in God—a God who not only can heal, but also restore and uphold.

Staying Resilient is *not* filled with hollow, pat answers for dealing with a life-threatening diagnosis. Rather, it offers real hope for survival—and for coming out on top of the pile, instead of under it. Each chapter (with the exception of Chapter 6) ends with questions that can help the reader apply the information shared in the chapter. (Note: The "Points to Consider" at the end of each chapter may be reproduced for use with small groups.) The first three chapters encourage the reader to open God's Word and seek His perspective on the challenges being faced. The final chapters assist the reader in developing a plan for moving forward—and for sharing one's story with others.

You may read this book on your own or with a small group. Either way, you won't be going through your situation alone. In the end, you will know that God is with you, step by step, helping you not only to survive, but to thrive.

PREFACE

not only a survivor but a thriver as well!

This is not a:

- Religious treatise
- Sermon
- Motivational or self-help exercise
- Medical resource

So, then, what is it?

A lighthouse. *Amen*

Think about it. A lighthouse does its work when the lights go out, when the sun sets, when it is dark.

The life purpose of a lighthouse is protection. It warns ships of possible and imminent dangerous waters or shorelines. The lighthouse offers a penetrating beacon when there are storms or dense fog. It is a beacon that can offer navigators a sense of bearing, perspective, and hope.

I am not a lighthouse, but what I want to share is designed to provide a beacon of hope and encouragement for people who need protection and a sense of bearing. I want my story to be a guiding light to those whose lives, plans, and futures have been seemingly capsized by a cancer or other diagnosis that medically offers little hope and much darkness.

Why did I write this, and for whom?

I initially wrote with the goal of helping other men in particular, as they cope with: (1) the fact that their wives have received cancer diagnoses; and (2) the fact that everything associated with those diagnoses is turning life upside down and sideways—from who picks up the kids and cooks the meals to the interruption or redefinition of sexual intimacy.

I wrote without an expressed "begin with the end in mind" concept (contrary to what Stephen R. Covey would say is habit #2 in his renowned book, *The 7 Habits of Highly Effective People*®).[1] As the content and sections unfolded, I began to share with others what I was writing, and several outcomes emerged. I was told (by men and women) this manuscript could be:

- A study guide that could be used by a church or community to assist patients or caregivers in general, regardless of sex
- A book
- A resource for a medical entity that provides cancer treatment
- All the above

Writing became an unexpected source of therapy and revelation to me—a reflection on a personal journey that was rarely smooth and often rocky, even though I may have disguised the turmoil. At the same time (to my amazement), I received encouragement from others (both men and women) whom God placed in my path—people whose loved ones also had been hit by cancer. Even though the content was unfinished, I felt led to share select portions with these individuals. The feedback was positive, gratifying, and humbling.

At the end of the day, as others read, listened, edited, critiqued, and guided me, it became clear I wanted to help other spouses and caregivers (both men and women). I was seeking to help them avoid the potholes that magnified my personal weaknesses and vulnerabilities—crevices that scarred me, my loved ones, and—most importantly—our relationships. I realized that if I moved forward with what had become my vision, other men and women might be in a better position than I had been (both emotionally and spiritually) to help their loved ones to thrive, not merely survive, as they entered uncharted waters.

My prayer and vision are that this book will help you, regardless of who you are—cancer patient, survivor, caregiver, or anyone struggling with another of life's curveballs.

God knows.

And that is what matters the most.

Lawrence (Larry) R. Blundred
Spring 2017

ACKNOWLEDGMENTS

I have so many people to thank, beginning with my amazing wife, Donna, "The Thriver." Donna read each word and page as it poured out of me in early 2016. She was patient with me as she sat in our den, while I perched myself at the kitchen counter and wrote ... walked and paced ... and wrote some more.

To my children, for their unique roles: Initially, to son Rob, for his feedback on the first draft, giving me perspective and insight that opened my eyes and has proven invaluable; to daughter Christine, for expressing a visual idea for the front cover that designer Dale Meyers liked and brought to life; and to son Phil, for taking time during work and wedding plans to sketch out logo ideas for Thriver Ministries, LLC.

Steve Kehoe and Tim Keller at Kehoe Financial Advisors, my employer since early 2007. They have encouraged and supported me and Donna personally from day one and provided excellent suggestions on content. I value their friendship and integrity.

Scott Dill, Kathy Beechem, and various ministers and staff members at Crossroads Church encouraged, blessed, and guided me.

Patrick Conlon, from the Crossroads West Side campus team, took time to teach me Dropbox. He edited and improved anything I sent him, and then he became an amazing friend and partner in starting a Cancer Support Group. Patrick is not just a third-party contributor. His lovely wife, Melanie, is a two-time cancer survivor, so he understands—and understood.

Margie Redford, my editor, has been so calm, patient, and wise. Her insight and encouragement will never be forgotten. She and her husband, Doug, reflect Christ to all that know them, despite the darts and arrows that life has thrown their way. When God brought Margie to mind as my editor, everything seemed to fall in place. We will see!

To the men and women of our first cancer support group at Crossroads Church, where I had the opportunity to share what I was doing and "test the waters," if you will. They are amazing survivors *and* thrivers.

To the publishers and artists with for <u>KING & COUNTRY</u> and Casting Crowns, for your generous hearts, enabling us to include the lyrics to two songs ("<u>Thrive</u>" and "<u>It's Not Over Yet</u>") in Appendix B of the book. You understood why these songs matter!

To the team at ScrogginsGrear Consultants and CPAs (Donna's former employer), and particularly, Terry Grear, for their and his support and encouragement, modeling the values that make this group unique. How many companies would bring in a sofa for their employee (Donna), enabling her, when needed, to take a nap?

Finally, to members of our Brave Journey Group through Crossroads, where the idea to write this book first germinated … and would not stop growing in my mind and heart, because you would not stop encouraging me!

INTRODUCTION

Hi there, Mrs. Bushy (my nickname for my wife, whose hair has come back as it was!),

As you know, Donna, as I begin to write I do not know where this will lead. By that, I mean that I do not have an intended place where this shows up or ends up. Perhaps it will be a published book that generates donations to a specific charity, or it may be used to support community or spiritual groups at our local church. Will it have a wide or very narrow audience? I have no idea. I have never written anything like this before—certainly never a book!

Candidly, I am fine with that premise for starters. I would rather not have my mind focused on something potentially big and grandiose, but on something very basic, simple, and from the heart. And that begins with a vision. No, not a supernova, supernatural knock-me-off-my-feet event, rather a voice from heaven directing me to go (or do)—NOW!

This sense of vision began marinating in my heart and mind in early 2016. To use a food analogy, several ingredients came together as in a recipe. Each was added at a different time and date. The finished stew, if you will, has given me a sense of comfort food and the courage to take a bite, and another, allowing others to taste and share too.

The first ingredient …

At each step, one ingredient seemed to complement the others in the cooking process. The first ingredient came in February as an idea. I saw a flyer for the annual University of Cincinnati Brain Tumor Center Wine Tasting Event. I recalled that, at recent events, brain tumor survivors had taken a few minutes to share about their journeys.

So why not see if my wife, Donna, could be invited to speak and share at this year's event? After all, she *is* a brain tumor survivor— and "Thriver" (my nickname for her since June 2012 when her brain tumor was diagnosed as a Grade IV glioblastoma). Need I say more? Most patients with such a diagnosis aren't alive two to three years later to talk about their experiences.

To make a long story short, despite the help given to us by our oncologist, Dr. Richard Curry, Donna was not included as a speaker for the event. But Dr. Ronald Warnick (Chair in Neurosurgical Oncology and Director of the UC Brain Tumor Center) did arrange for Donna to be interviewed by Cindy Starr, a staff journalist/writer. Cindy wrote an amazing article, posted on both the Walk Ahead and Neuroscience websites of the Brain Tumor Center. (Note: When you're finished reading this introduction, be sure to read Donna's story. We've included it in Appendix A.) Since that article, we have received much positive feedback—from both those who are receiving and giving care, women and men alike. (Don't lose what I just said about *men*.)

Next, add …

The second ingredient in the "stew" was the Brave Journey at Crossroads Church with our small group. In the group setting, we are challenged to create a heading, a direction, a vision—something we are saying personally and publicly that we want to pursue, to change. It may be to change jobs or a career, move to start a business, or overcome an addiction.

In my case, after three drafts, my vision became clear: "To explore and consider transition from my current full-time employment to something in the next year that includes ministry, where I could help and serve men whose spouses have been diagnosed with cancer." I was not certain how this would be done, but it was my heading, my vision.

And finally, …

The third, and perhaps most pungent ingredient, was introduced to the recipe when Crossroads Church (West Side Campus) gathered to visit the CityLink Center as part of our Brave Journey. CityLink, located in Cincinnati, Ohio, is a city-wide initiative that offers integrated services to help people break free from poverty and find hope. There, getting a bite to eat before the journey began, Donna and I saw Artie Kuhn and his wife, Lisa. We had not seen Artie in over ten years. We first met Artie before he was married. He was one of the founding leaders of the Young Life chapter at Oak Hills High School near our home. We initiated the formation of this chapter and served on the Young Life advisory committee for several years.

As Donna told her story to Artie and Lisa, Lisa shared that she'd lost two family members who had the same form of brain tumor as Donna's. Lisa also said that her supervisor, Kathy Beechem, had written a book following the loss of her husband to—you guessed it (and of course, it was very sad to say and repeat)—the same form of brain cancer. *So Far, So Good: A Memoir of a Brain Tumor Patient and His Caregiver*[1] is a positive and inspiring, but real and tough, testimony written about Kathy's beloved husband, Pete Nadherny.

Right then and there, my vision was crystalized. It became more vivid and real when, in a separate room at CityLink, we were presented with various phrases or words that might describe our journey to where God was leading us. I immediately selected the phrase, "I have a vision for you." The supporting verse was Jeremiah 33:3: "Call to me and I will answer you and tell you great and unsearchable things you do not know."

That did it. A final confirmation came when Lisa Kuhn said, "I would really like you to meet Kathy." Two weeks later, that meeting took place. I talked and shared with Kathy for over an hour. Without any plan or premise on my part, that meeting may have opened other doors. Only God knows. The timing and outcome are His.

The Timing and Vision

I write this while Donna is still thriving, despite the odds and medical diagnosis. When I finish the writing, I fully expect she will still be living and thriving. I write this now because I know that it may be harder to write if Donna's condition were to reverse. The unknown future does not dominate my thoughts, but writing this now enables us to work together, and, while the content and process is challenging, I believe it will help to engage both of us mentally and spiritually. The thoughts and encouragements found in this writing could apply to any spouse whose mate has been diagnosed with a potentially life-threatening disease, but my vision is to speak especially to men.

Why Men?—Initially

I do this because I believe men, perhaps, are more vulnerable to stumble and fail. Men (myself included) are more dependent upon our spouses than we are willing to admit. We are prone to "fix now, no help needed, thank you very much!"

Recently, I was standing in line at a Dunkin' Donuts. A grocery store was next door. In front of me was a young mother with three very young daughters, one in her arms. The mother was not having an easy time. She was explaining to her children the day's plan: "You know how Daddy hates to shop, so we'll each get a donut. Then we'll get groceries and pick up some plants. We can all plant flowers and make a garden today. Sound fun?"

I suspect that others who overheard the conversation smiled and thought, *This plan sounded great!* But I couldn't stop myself from thinking about the father. How his life would change if his wife was diagnosed with a cancer such as Donna's! *He* may become the one holding the kids, learning to buy groceries, buying plants—and perhaps planting them with his wife's supervision, but no direct or physical support. He also may be the one ordering her medications, transporting her to chemotherapy or radiation treatments, or arranging for others to step in and help with these arrangements so he can go to work. And he may not like this new role that has suddenly and unexpectedly been thrust upon his world. He may have to learn to cook. (Or he may decide to rely instead on carry-out or heat-and-serve foods.) He may say, "Who cares about plants and a garden!"

While no one can know or fully anticipate how he or she will respond if a spouse suffers with a life-threatening cancer, I believe men may struggle more in this unexpected role than women. In fact, a man may say (or think), "Who cares" about a lot of things—not just whether the family gets tomatoes from the garden or grocery store.

On the lighter side . . .

It seems God knew that men would need help—and a helper. God knew that most men would be lost without a helpmate. A good friend of mine, Gil Linz, always tells a closing joke in his role as moderator of a monthly networking event that I attend. Recently, Gil shared with us "The Top 5 Reasons God Created Eve":

#5: God was worried that Adam would frequently become lost in the garden because he refused to ask for directions.

#4: God knew that one day Adam would require someone to locate and hand him the remote.

#3: God knew Adam would never go out and buy himself a new fig leaf when his wore out, and would therefore need Eve to buy one for him.

#2: God knew if the world was to be populated, men would never be able to handle the pain and discomfort of childbearing.

Finally, the #1 reason why God created Eve? (Most men will admit the truth to this, I hope.) **When God finished the creation of Adam, He stepped back, scratched His head, and said, "I can do better than that!"**[2]

(If this did not bring a smile, you are having a bad day—or you are not married yet!)

His golfing or biking buddies may offer condolences or kind words ("Hey, let me know how I can help"), but his time golfing and hanging out with his buds may be seriously curtailed. He may begin to feel isolated and alone. He may ask himself, *Is this what it feels like when you are depressed or anxious?*

The other thing this young father would be trying to do is "fix" the situation. He is wired this way. He can't help it. After weeks and months of treatments and seeing his beautiful wife wearing a scarf or hat in public to cover her hairless head, he feels helpless. He privately talks to the doctor to explore what else can be done. He wonders if he should bring up the idea of a wig. He calls some of his wife's friends to see whether they can stop by more often so he can play golf and join his buddies at a game, after a game, or at a restaurant. If he has family in town, he wonders if he should ask them to watch the girls more often?

I wondered whether this father would have a group of men from his church community who would offer real support, not just words. Men who would step in to both challenge and suggest, encourage, and be the hands and feet of Christ for him. Men who know that we are all broken, and that brokenness is not the end, but perhaps the beginning of a breakthrough. When we can't fix something like cancer or the way it affects our spouses, I believe men, more than women, are most vulnerable to potentially-destructive thoughts, behaviors, and outcomes. I know this firsthand, and that is why I started writing with men in mind.

⊕ brokenness is perhaps the beginning of a breakthrough!

At the same time, during this journey, God has allowed me to meet several women who are also struggling as they assume new caregiver roles or take on duties previously handled by their husbands. I have shared several sections of this book with these women, and they have thanked me. So I would be shortsighted to focus solely on men, and limit what God might do with this content.

But I can only speak for myself—and some of the men God has placed in my path since June 2012. Throughout the journey, many men have stepped in and stepped up to listen, encourage, pray, challenge, and support me in ways that I will never forget. Now I want to give back—first to these men who have stood by me, and also to men I have never met or may never meet. And if even one man approaches me in the future and says, "Thank you for writing this," it will be worth it.

In what form or fashion will this happen?
I do not know. That's God's call.

This is my vision.

This is my hope.

But vision is worthless without taking risk or action. So I take this step, out of the boat and onto the water. I do so with faith that God will lead and guide me.

As I write this, Hebrews 11:1 comes to mind. Although stated differently in various Bible translations, I believe the key words are *confidence*, *assurance*, and *substance*.

- "Now faith is *confidence* in what we hope for and *assurance* about what we do not see" (NIV).
- "Now faith is the *assurance* of things hoped for, the conviction of things not seen" (NASB).
- "Now faith is the *substance* of things hoped for, the evidence of things not seen" (KJV).

With these key words in mind, may you continue *your* journey and not just survive … but thrive!

[handwritten margin notes: Wow! This is my Verse. from my High School Years.]

1
FACING THE FACTS

"Not forgiving is like drinking rat poison and expecting the rat to die."[1]

—Anne Lamott

" we must forgive in order to live / thrive "

Bes TZC

Anger is big business. Read up on it. It's depressing. It will make you angry!

When people get angry, or hold onto anger, it can have serious medical consequences. Anger can cause depression, contribute to strokes and heart disease, trigger high blood pressure, and more. It becomes big business for doctors, hospitals, pharmacies, pharmaceutical companies, psychologists, and counselors who benefit from a greater demand for their services.

So why would anyone with half a brain choose to hold onto anger?

Because we are human.

We grew up in homes where angry outbursts were the norm.

We have contentious personalities or are very competitive and hate to lose.

Or, life has thrown us nightmare outcomes or diagnoses that can't be sugar-coated. Our minds and emotions spin, and we end up on the anger roller coaster.

Face it—at some point in this process you have been angry or bitter, or both. In your mind or in practice, you have yelled, screamed, cussed, or pounded a wall in anger. Or as I did, you may have tossed your cookies and openly expressed your anger at God.

You would prefer not to be feeling as you do, but you do.

The shortest verse in the Bible is "Jesus wept" (John 11:35). Jesus showed emotions—joy, amazement, disappointment, sorrow, and anger. Maybe it wasn't the kind of anger we are feeling now, but when Jesus entered the temple courts and drove out all who were buying and selling there, He was not in a Sermon-on-the-Mount frame of mind. Although Matthew doesn't use the word *anger* to describe what was happening, it sure sounds like it. "[Jesus] overturned the tables of the money changers and the benches of those selling doves" (Matthew 21:12).

So, what is anger? Can it ever be positive or healthy?

My Perspective

I think you *know* when you are angry, or you hear someone say they are angry. Anger usually has a focus, a target. Someone or something triggers the adverse feeling. Yes, anger may be hiding other emotions, such as fear or sadness. But anger surfaces, nonetheless, and from my personal experience, anger finds a "home," or a response.

When you see a tornado on TV, you watch in amazement. When you see, hear, or feel it first-hand, your response is different. The latter is called fear and panic. If you survive the tornado but lose everything, including some of your friends and family, you may at first feel shock or agony. The emotion of anger may surface later. But anger toward *what* or *whom*? Mother Nature? God? A life that is not fair?

When you hear that your spouse has a life-threatening cancer, anger may be triggered immediately, or it may be deferred. I was talking with a friend recently about anger. He told me how a young couple at his church had come forward to ask for prayer. The husband shared that he been diagnosed with a rapidly-spreading cancer in his liver. His wife openly admitted to everyone that she no longer had any use for God. She cried and made it clear that she was mad at and angry with God. And there was more to this young lady's story. Prior to meeting her husband, she had been engaged to her first true love. Before the wedding date, he was diagnosed with a brain tumor and died a few months later. Why would God let this happen—twice?

As I write this, the sister-in-law of one of my best friends is suffering from a rare and rapidly-spreading internal melanoma cancer. She is not expected to live much longer. Her husband is a pastor. He was married before. His first wife also died of cancer.

So, if the young lady and the pastor are or become angry with God, is their anger justified? I don't have a corner on the truth to answer that question. The reality is that we *do* become angry, and prolonged anger is not what we seek or welcome. Anger can tear us up physically and emotionally. It can be a slow drip of poison, affecting how we live our lives and interact with others.

I believe the real question is how we handle it. How do we live with it? How do we get beyond anger? If someone unexpectedly lights a match in front of our faces, we will all respond in the same way. We will flinch and our heads will pop back, pronto. But not everyone handles or responds to adversity or unexpected bad news in the same way.

I recall the first time I walked into the room where Donna was recovering in intensive care following her surgery. She had bandages covering her entire head and face, and tubes and monitors sticking out of each arm. Two of her friends were standing next to her. I stood at the door with tears pouring out. Then I collapsed into the arms of Karen and Deb.

I was not angry. I was shocked, stunned. I knew this was going to be bad. But not until I was there in the room could I grasp the extent of what had just happened.

You probably won't understand my reaction—unless you are there. It's like trying to identify with a family being interviewed on TV whose home has been flattened by a tornado. You can't fully comprehend the feelings expressed, unless it is *your* home that has been devastated.

About a week later, we received the diagnosis on the tumor. It was a number 10 earthquake, one that takes down buildings and bridges and lives—a Grade IV glioblastoma. The tumor had been removed. But it was what the associate to Donna's surgeon told us that first triggered real, definitive anger in my stomach: "This cancer always comes back. I am so sorry."

Those simple words changed me.

words are so powerful - they can change a person = Simple words can change a man or women!

A nurse had ushered my daughter, Christine, and me to a room adjacent to Donna's. That's where the prediction was shared. I became unmistakably bitter, frustrated, and—yes—angry. In my mind (uttered to no one), I was angry with God. I started grinding my teeth and breathing fiercely through my nostrils. I stood up and glared out the window. Christine uttered just four words: "A child's worst nightmare."

I remember driving home that night. The Christian radio station K-LOVE popped on when I turned on the car. I immediately and firmly turned off the station. And for close to two years afterward, unless I was in church where I could not turn off the music, I did not listen to Christian music.

Even when Donna got back home, if K-LOVE was on when I sat down behind the wheel and started the car, I turned it off or changed the station. What is amazing is that Donna said nothing. She knew I was angry, and I had told her that I was angry with God.

At that time, she was the only one who knew.

She—and God!

On his website, gotquestions.org, S. Michael Houdmann offers this answer to the question, Is it wrong to be angry with God?

"Being angry at God is something that people have wrestled with throughout time. When something tragic happens in our lives, we ask God the question, 'Why?' because it is our natural response. What we are really asking Him, though, is not so much 'Why, God?' as 'Why *me*, God?' This response indicates two flaws in our thinking. First, as believers, we operate under the impression that life should be easy, and that God should prevent tragedy from happening to us.

When He does not, we get angry with Him. Second, when we do not understand the extent of God's sovereignty, we lose confidence in His ability to control circumstances, other people, and the way they affect us. Then we get angry with God because He seems to have lost control of the universe, and especially, control of our lives. When we lose faith in God's sovereignty, it is because our frail human flesh is grappling with our own frustration and our lack of control over events. When good things happen, we all too often attribute it to our own achievements and success. When bad things happen, however, we are quick to blame God, and we get angry with Him for not preventing it, which indicates the first flaw in our thinking—that we deserve to be immune to unpleasant circumstances.

Tragedies bring home the awful truth that we are not in charge. All of us think at one time or another that we can control the outcomes of situations, but in reality, it is God who is in charge of all of His creation. Everything that happens is either caused by or allowed by God. Not a sparrow falls to the ground, nor a hair from our head, without God knowing about it (Matthew 10:29-31). ...

Does God understand when we are angry, frustrated, or disappointed with Him? Yes, He knows our hearts and He knows how difficult and painful life in this world can be. ...

Can we trust God with everything, our very lives and the lives of our loved ones? Of course, we can! Our God is compassionate, full of grace and love, and we can trust Him with all things. When tragedies happen to us, we know God can use them to bring us closer to Him and to strengthen our faith, bringing us to maturity and completeness (Psalm 34:18; James 1:2-4). Then, we can be a comforting testimony to others (2 Corinthians 1:3-5)."[2] (Used by permission.)

CHAPTER 1 POINTS TO CONSIDER

Key Points
- When people get angry, or hold onto anger, it can have serious consequences.
- Face it—at some point in this process you have been angry or bitter, or both.
- When you hear that your spouse has a life-threatening cancer, anger may be triggered immediately, or it may be deferred.
- How we deal with anger.

God's Perspective

very much a foundational truth + keys to freedom....

Check out Ephesians 4:25-27. ⟵

"Therefore each of you must put off falsehood and speak truthfully to your neighbor, for we are all members of one body. 'In your anger, do not sin:' Do not let the sun go down while you are still angry, and do not give the devil a foothold."

- Who is your neighbor? (See Jesus' answer to this question in Luke 10:25–37.)

- Is there a connection between the anger we hold on to and our being more likely to sin?

- What other sins can emerge if we are angry with God?
  - a hard heart
  - pride
  - addictions
  - idolatry
  - disobedience
  - lack of repentance

- How can the devil get a foothold, and in what way might he exploit us?

- through choice of sinnful thoughts & actions.
- through works of flesh
- separates us from our relationship w/ Christ.

Your Perspective

- How do these verses from Ephesians 4 speak to you?

They remind me regarding facing my emotions.
Why I am angry + to deal w/ it.
To repent and release this anger.

- What are you angry about?

I am so angry about the way my daughter
has rewritten history! She has mis-led
lied about many many many times + issues.

- How are you doing in the area of anger?

not as good as I thought!

- Is it possible that anger can be a friend, or is it always a foe? Defend your answer. *It can be a friend - by putting a name on the deeper issue which is hurt, and abuse of another person! A misunderstanding.*

- Rate yourself regarding anger:

___ I've got this covered.

___ Not sure. It's a roller coaster.

_X_ I need help.

- Based on your rating above, why did you answer as you did?

2
MAKING A DIFFERENCE

"One person can make a difference, and everyone should try."[1]
—President John F. Kennedy

What do you have in common with Judy Hopps of the animated Disney film *Zootopia*? Plenty.

Officer Judy Hopps is the first bunny to join Zootopia's police department. She jumps at the chance to crack a case, even if it means teaming up with a small-time fox with a big mouth. Judy lives out resiliency. She is told that her size limitations will also limit her ability to succeed. She is assigned to parking meter duty—the equivalent of cleaning toilets or peeling potatoes at a fast-food restaurant. While carrying out her assigned duties, Judy meets the con-artist fox, who later becomes her friend and ally in solving a case that no one else, not even the Chief of Police, could solve. Judy does not give up or give in. She reminds us both in word and deed that, yes, life often is unfair and messy. But at the same time, she sticks to the overriding motive that made her want to become a police officer: To make the world a better place, no matter what life deals you. To push on, despite difficult circumstances, or what we perceive (or are told) to be limitations.

I want to tell you about a Judy Hopps in my life. His name is Rick Iles. I have known Rick and his family since the early 1980s. We first met when Rick and his wife, Terri, visited the church we were attending. We were hosting a small group, and they joined us. A friendship soon formed. Rick taught the men's class at our church.

When you leave a group of any kind, no matter what you say, connections and contacts aren't the same. That's what happened here. But we still attended their children's weddings, and we regularly exchanged Christmas cards.

The distanced relationship changed when we learned that Rick, who was a public-school teacher, had received a diagnosis of Parkinson's disease. Rick did the best he could, but ultimately, he had to retire early, in his late 50s. This hit Rick and his family hard. He struggled to walk and was advised not to drive. That's when we started meeting up again, just to talk. No agenda. We would share and pray—always at his home.

But the day after Donna and I were told, "That type of cancer always comes back," Rick showed up, cane in hand. He'd driven himself to the hospital. That was (and is) Rick Iles. We met in a private waiting room. He just listened and patted my shoulder when I cried. He prayed for me and then returned to Donna's room to pray for her.

If there is a man I know who is not a pastor but has the heart and soul of one, it is Rick. As I walked out with him, Rick said something that I would hear from many well-meaning men and visitors: "Larry, I will call you. We will meet soon."

But that is exactly what Rick did. Persistently. Consistently.

Truth is, I was not ready to meet with Rick or others who might want to talk with me, pray for me, or offer support. When Donna left the hospital four weeks later, my focus was on her, adjusting to what she could do—and not do. I was assuming the role of caregiver and taking on household duties that I had depended on Donna to do ever since we were married.

But Rick would call regularly, just to touch base. To say a prayer. To tell us he and Terri were praying for us. All during this time, the challenges associated with the Parkinson's (and his medications) were intensifying. Rick was struggling in many ways as well, but he never relented.

We finally did meet up again in person. Over the past three years, because Rick reached out and was persistent, the depth of our friendship has deepened. There are things each of us know or have shared that only we know. We trust each other. And we are better men for it.

My Perspective
Some of you reading this will understand exactly what I am sharing. Some of you may not. You may not have a Rick Iles in your life. You may never have been a Rick Iles to another friend or neighbor. One thing for sure, Rick taught me several lessons that were reinforced when I sought professional counsel during this time:
- God can and still does use people who have flaws or perceive that they are unworthy.

- We are refreshed, healed, and restored when we reach out and help others who have the same (or similar) needs and issues that we have.
- Others will open up and share and become vulnerable when *we* do the same—and when we do so in a confidential manner and without judgement.

I've learned something else that is amazing to me: You will find men and women everywhere who need help and who are sending out radar signals, if you just pay attention, listen, and ask some good questions. God will make your paths cross, if you have your eyes, ears, and heart open—*and* if you are willing to do something about it. The latter is key!

I write this on Memorial Day Weekend 2016. Before the Saturday service at Crossroads West Side, a staff associate introduced me to his friend, Dan, who has been hit with a rare blood disorder that affects only one in 1,000 people. This disease causes organ failure. Even though the disease is officially in remission, chemotherapy regimens and the disorder itself have caused him to suffer with Stage D congestive heart failure, severe weakness, shortness of breath, and anemia.

Earlier in the week before we met, Dan was at his cardiologist for a regular visit. The nurse practitioner had given up on him after not being able to take his pulse manually. An EKG revealed Dan was in atrial fibrillation and he was admitted to Christ Hospital immediately. For a while they were not able to detect a pulse and it appeared Dan might pass away from congestive heart failure.

To the surprise of Dan's friend and Pastor Greg (both of whom were called to Christ Hospital in Cincinnati when circumstances appeared dire), Dan walked into that Saturday service. His son had driven him. Dan's friend brought him over to me. He knew my wife's story. He knew my story. He wanted me to connect with Dan.

For fifteen minutes, Dan and I talked. I did not seek out Dan, but I sensed there was a purpose and a direction for our meeting. I asked Dan if he would like to meet again. I gave him my mobile number, and after the service, he sent me a text with the times and dates he was available to meet—that week!

I arrived at Dan's home at the agreed-upon time and was greeted at the front door. Attached to Dan's nose was a mask connected to a breathing device with a long cord that enabled him to walk around without being confined. (You get a picture of the length of that cord!) I soon learned that Dan has lost 30 pounds. He has a very restrictive diet. Dan loves God and Jesus. He talks about the Bible verses he recites to crowd out negative thoughts. He believes in prayer and believes he will be healed. So does his wife, Ann, who joined us, and so do I. We prayed earnestly. I believe God has placed Dan and Ann in our lives for a reason.

Dan and Ann wanted to meet *this* lady—Donna, "The Thriver."

Why? Because we are in the "hope" business. That's it in a nutshell.

So, the four of us *did* meet. And we have met and conversed many times since. Months later, Dan is still fighting and much more than just surviving. His accomplishments are largely because of his spirit and the persistent work of Ann, who continues to explore every medical option at any facility—from the Mayo Clinic in Rochester, MN, to Boston, MA.

I do not know if there is (or ever will be) a Dan in your life. I do know that your problems and issues—however real and painful they are—will be somehow softened and put in perspective when God places a Dan, or a Rick Iles, in your life.

Blessings always go both ways. But you need to be looking and listening, ready to receive them. We need Ricks and Dans, and they need us. It's true—each of us can make a difference when we determine to push on, despite our limiting circumstances. (Thank you, Judy Hopps!)

Update on Dan and Ann (from Larry):

Dan and Ann, at this writing in mid-July 2017, are residing at the Nazarene Well House in Rochester, MN. This enables Dan immediate access to the medical team and resources at St. Mary's Hospital nearby. St. Mary's is part of the Mayo Clinic network. Dan needs specialized care, and both of them need our prayers.

In the past five months, this couple has been on a physical and emotional roller coaster. They have modeled resiliency, not just once, but over and over again.

Yes, Dan faces physical and emotional challenges associated with this rare condition. But he is fighting, and Ann's refusal to give up has resulted in Dan being in a better position now to survive—and hopefully thrive.

I decided to add this update after talking with both Dan and Ann yesterday. I learned something that encouraged me. I was aware Dan was writing a book of his own; he has completed a first draft and has turned it over to Ann and his daughter for comments and editing.

So, I am going to step out now, Dan. I am going to send you the proceeds from the first 33 books sold, so you can use those funds as needed—to help pay for an official editor, to take a little side trip with Ann, or pay some medical bills. Dan and Ann, this is not about calling attention to me. I just feel led to do this because we love you. We miss you. If possible, we want to visit you, still believing in our hearts that your condition will improve and that you, indeed, will be back in Cincinnati soon!

And, maybe you, the reader, will feel led to help as well. If so, you can contact me via www.thriverministries.com or via e-mail: thriverministries@gmail.com. Put "Dan and Ann" in the subject line.

I know you will respect their privacy, but join us in praying for both Dan and Ann.

CHAPTER 2 POINTS TO CONSIDER

Key Points

- You can make a difference, no matter what life deals you.
- God can and still does use people to help other people.
- You will find men and women everywhere who need help, if you are paying attention—and are willing to do something about it.

God's Perspective

Check out Hebrews 10:24, 25:

"Let us consider how we may spur one another on toward love and good deeds, not giving up meeting together, as some are in the habit of doing, but encouraging one another—and all the more as you see the Day approaching."

Read Romans 1:11, 12. Notice how Paul speaks from his heart. Catch the words he uses and the passion there (emphasis mine):

"I **long** to see you so that I may **impart** to you some spiritual gift to make you **strong**—that is, that you **and** I may be **mutually encouraged** by each other's faith."

- How do these passages express different, but complementary, themes and ideas?

- What do you think it means to "spur one another on"? Don't spurs hurt?

- Why do you think meeting together is emphasized?

- What spiritual gifts might people need to become strong when they are feeling weak? (Consider the fruit of the Spirit mentioned in Galatians 5:22, 23.)

Your Perspective
- How do the verses from Hebrews and Romans speak to you where you are right now?

- What are some ways others could encourage you at this time?

- Think of people you know who you believe need help or encouragement. Write their names here.

- How might you encourage these people?

- So what are you going to do—and when?

- Who will benefit from what you have decided to do? How will this benefit them?

3
CHOOSING YOUR COURSE

"Although the world is full of suffering,
it is full also of the overcoming of it."[1]
—Helen Keller

On August 5, 2015, I arrived at Rick Iles's home for one of our meetings. We started catching up on events that had taken place since our last visit. Rick pulled out a note that his wife, Terri, had penned for both Donna and me. It began with the above quote from Helen Keller, and then continued:

> *"Suffering will either be your master or your servant, depending on how you handle the crisis of life. After all, a crisis doesn't make a person; it reveals what a person is made of. What life does to us depends on what life finds in us."*
>
> *Rick and Terri, 8/5/2015*

In recent months, Rick and I had talked increasingly about suffering—the unknowable and unanswerable parts of it. We had plenty of questions: Why did Rick's father die of bone cancer at such an early age? Why do some people survive traumatic accidents and others do not? Why did a friend of ours, Dr. Mike Wood, who was diagnosed with the same GMB tumor six months after Donna's diagnosis, die two years later, while Donna continues on her journey? Why did the husband of Donna's former supervisor die in his 50s after a four-year struggle with a cancer that first showed up in his neck and eventually spread? Why are seemingly healthy and thriving people like Rick and Donna diagnosed with potentially life-threatening diseases or cancers? They have never been seriously sick, period!

I asked Rick if he ever asked himself or God, "Why *me*?"

"Yes, I have, and still do." His answer was simple—and honest.

I recall that this particular day was not a good one for Rick. Doses of his medication had been adjusted, and he was shaking more. I looked at my friend, as I have so many times looked at my wife, and asked myself, *Why not me? Why am I healthy?* Except for a couple of surgeries on my ankle and back, I have no physical or cognitive issues that limit me. Sure, I have aches and pains, but no limitations. None of this makes sense, does it?

Further, Rick used to be a guy that could have replaced Tim Allen on the TV show *Home Improvement*. Rick still has all the knowledge and drive, but there are no more ladders for Rick. He used to climb on roofs and hang out of windows. Not now.

This is what is so unique: Donna and Rick still enjoy talking tools and projects. They worked together on projects at the church we attended. They would trade ideas and share tips. When we installed stages and platforms for the annual Christmas program, Donna was there with all the other guys—tool belt and drill in hand, giving directions and overseeing the process. She knew where everything was stored and how it all came together.

But since her surgery and recovery, Donna has not touched two of her favorite "sports": power drills and saws *and* her sewing machine. She misses those. She could always create, repair, and build, whether it was a dress for daughter Christine or a LEGO® table for the boys. When she wanted a new outfit, she would rarely buy one. She would make it.

So how could a loving God do this to her—and to Rick?

My Perspective

The type of questions mentioned above may never be answered on this Earth. But if we base our belief in God on a prerequisite need to have the answers, we will end up in the camp that sees life as futile and without purpose or meaning. We may believe there is no God or, if He ever existed, to us, He is dead.

So, at some point I believe we have a clear choice—fight or flight.

What do I mean?

I mean that when everyone else believes there is no hope and, therefore, no reason to fight, we must cultivate an atmosphere that challenges the flight plan or outcome carved out by others.

Is this easy? Does it make sense?

No! Absolutely not—to both questions.

So why bother? The doctors say, "Six months, at best." "The treatments, if successful, can add three to six months to her life expectancy." "Even if all the tumor has been removed, it always comes back." "There is no cure for Parkinson's."

And on and on and on.

Even during my greatest internal mess, my highest level of being ticked off at God, I told Rick Iles on that first visit, "The doctors do not know Donna."

If she can believe there is _____, then there can be _____.

What word is missing here?

HOPE.

Next to love, HOPE is the greatest, most powerful word ever created. HOPE is a word that rides the back of the future. A future without hope is, well, hopeless. There is no reason to fight or go on.

So, even though I had turned off the Christian music (and eventually, everything else Christian unless forced upon me by sitting in a church service), I never forgot one of Donna's favorite songs, "Thrive," by Casting Crowns. Consider the lyrics of the first verse and chorus. (Note: The complete lyrics are included for you in Appendix B.)

Verse 1

Here in this worn and weary land where many a dream has died,
like a tree planted by the water, we never will run dry.
So, living water flowing through, God, we thirst for more of You.
Fill our hearts, and flood our souls with one desire.

Chorus
Just to know you, and to make You known.
We lift Your name on high.
Shine like the sun; make darkness run and hide.
We know we were made for so much more
Than ordinary lives.
It's time for us to more than just survive.
We were made to thrive.

"Made to thrive." That was the hope Donna and I needed to be reminded of every day. I am not artistically inclined, but I can paint in words a vision of what I want to see. My vision was scenes of trees reaching to the skies—thriving. Or an active, energetic dog springing and jumping over a barrier—thriving. I shared my thoughts with others. Then Jill Grear, who works for

Donna's former employer, put her creativity to work. Soon "Donna, the Thriver" artwork was born—and hope could be seen.

I brought some flowers to the hospital with one of the pieces Jill had created. When Donna returned home, there were new "Donna, the Thriver" posters in the kitchen and near Donna's mirror in the bedroom.

Did these pictures make a difference for Donna? Honestly, I do not know. I do believe the artwork made more of a difference for me. I think I needed to see this message of hope more than Donna did. Why? Because, candidly, I did not have the thriving hope that she did. But I knew I could not let her see or feel doubt and fear in me.

So, regardless of where you are in your journey with your spouse or loved one, remember that you are, first and foremost, on a journey with God. I recall two points from messages given by Brian Tome and Chuck Mingo during the Brave Journey message series at Crossroads Church. Brian said, "God wants to make us holy, not happy." Chuck said (using the word picture of what happens to a tree that is constantly hit by strong winds), "Like distressed wood, a brave life is strengthened by storms."

The truth is, none of this is easy. In fact, it can be miserable. You may hear yourself saying, "Why bother?" or "Why fight?"

One of my favorite US presidents is Abraham Lincoln (and not just because I am from Illinois). I admire Lincoln mostly because he overcame such personal and professional adversity in his life. You could make a good argument that if Lincoln had not been president when he was, our nation would be much different today. And not in a good way.

It is not clear if Mr. Lincoln was a super-religious man with any strong church ties. But I love his honesty when he said, "I have been driven many times upon my knees by the overwhelming conviction that I had nowhere else to go. My own wisdom and that of all about me seemed insufficient for that day."[2]

Does that speak to you as it did to me?

We can choose to get on our knees.

We can choose to get on the phone with or in front of men God has placed in our path.

We can choose to be honest with ourselves.

We can choose to continue to fight.

OR, we can take flight, choosing to escape into behavior or a frame of mind that is destructive to both us and others.

And let's be honest—we know what the latter choice can lead to.

CHAPTER 3 POINTS TO CONSIDER

Key Points
- Suffering includes the unknowable and unanswerable.
- Basing our belief in God on the need to have all our questions answered is destructive.
- We must cultivate an atmosphere that challenges flight and chooses to fight.
- Finding hope is key. A life without hope is hopeless.
- First and foremost, you are on a journey with God. What you make of the journey is your choice.

God's Perspective—and Yours
Check out Jeremiah 29:11, 12:
"For I know the plans I have for you," declares the LORD, "plans to prosper you and not to harm you, plans to give you hope and a future. Then you will call on me and come and pray to me, and I will listen to you."

- What are some of the key words in these verses?

- Why do those words speak to you?

- How do these words and the remaining verses from Jeremiah 29 speak to you?

Read Psalm 25:4, 5:

"Show me your ways, LORD, teach me your paths. Guide me in your truth and teach me, for you are God my Savior, and my hope is in you all day long."

Ask yourself the same three questions for these verses.
• What are some of the key words in these verses?

• Why do those words speak to you?

• How do these words and the verses speak to you?

Read the passages from Jeremiah 29 and Psalm 25 again.
• What ideas or reminders are present in each set of verses?

• How do these verses speak to you about continuing to fight?

4
DEFINING YOUR "COPING" DEFAULTS

"If you think you're having a bad day, try missing one."
—My dad's mother and my grandmother, Agnes Blundred

So what good are those refrigerator magnets now?

You know what I mean. The one that says, "Life isn't about waiting for the storm to pass. It's about learning how to dance in the rain." Or, how about the magnet that says, "I don't need self-help, I need God's help"?

Aren't those just perfect for now? Just meditate on this or that and "it is well, it is well, with my soul."

While the magnets may seem trite at a time such as this, they do carry some truth. But will these sayings stuck on a refrigerator carry you while you are in a valley of doubt or depression? Or when your sleep patterns are so messed up that you feel tired all the time? Or (like the reference to Mr. Lincoln in chapter 3) when you are on your knees?

Do we simply need to buy more refrigerator magnets for the home and the office?

Will that do it?

In my opinion, no. It won't.

But I do believe there is a lesson to be learned from the magnets. Refrigerator magnets have an influence by repeating their message day after day. In the same way, what we repeatedly say to ourselves about what is happening around us or in our lives impacts us. I have found that the mind is a funny thing. It believes what it is told. You tend to become what you think about. And what you believe often happens.

Say *what*?!

Yes. Your physical health, body weight, and nutritional profile are dictated by the food you eat. Your mental health is a product of what you feed your mind—the things you allow your eyes to see and your ears to hear. The eyes and ears are the gatekeepers of your mind and thoughts, and ultimately (and most importantly), your core—your heart.

The Bible speaks openly and honestly about the heart:
"The heart is deceitful above all things and beyond cure. Who can understand it?" (Jeremiah 17:9).
"Where your treasure is, there your heart will be also" (Matthew 6:21).

So, if collecting magnets isn't the answer, what *can* we do to keep our world from collapsing?

My Perspective

I want to share three practical pointers (or defaults) that can help you focus on staying mind and heart healthy during this time of adjustment and transition. One definition given by *Merriam-Webster's* for *default* is "a selection made usually automatically or without active consideration due to lack of a viable alternative." The defaults I'm going to suggest are options that, once developed, your mind will go to automatically when you're trying to cope with the things life is throwing at you. Otherwise, your default may become pride, which is a false guide. It says: "I can handle this myself."

When I refer to a pointer, I want you to picture a dog—the Pointer. Pointers are an incredible breed of dogs. They are known for their dignity, sensibility, and style. They can be both loving *and* mischievous. But hunting trips are where Pointers truly shine. They have speed and stamina. They are determined. Those of you who have ever hunted with a Pointer know that. These dogs point to the target, to the reason you are hunting, whether it is downed ducks or pheasants or quail.

And so, our hunt begins.

Pointer 1: Prayer

The first pointer is prayer. What does prayer mean to you? Does it matter? Do you pray more when the waters in your life are normal and calm or when they are stormy? And how do you pray? And when?

Here's my take on prayer as it relates to where you might be right now. It's very simple: Don't overcomplicate prayer. Just follow the words of 1 Thessalonians 5:17: "Pray continually."

What does this mean? Allow me to share a personal perspective on praying continually. Prior to Donna's diagnosis, my prayers were perfunctory. A quick prayer at dinner or, on occasion, with Donna at bedtime. If there was bad news about a friend or my parents' health, the prayers became more deep and emotional. But there was no passion. The prayers were shallow. How do I know that? Am I being too hard on myself? After all, at least I prayed, right?

The shallow and perfunctory nature of my prayer life hit home when I had something really *serious* to pray about—my wife's health and life. Now, prayers mattered. I was not just speaking words, but pleading.

I can remember the first day I returned to the office to pick up mail and check in with coworkers. Donna was still in the hospital. I walked into my office. There was a pile of mail in my inbox. I sat down and faced the TV screen where I could see a daily stream of financial news from CNBC. I robotically turned on the TV, then turned on my computer and started thumbing through my e-mails. At that moment, I just lost it. Suddenly, none of these things mattered.

For the first time in many years, I just dropped to my knees, put my head and hands in my chair and started crying. I was alone. But we all know I was not. I remember what I said because these were words I would repeat over and over, aloud or to myself, every day: "Jesus, please heal Donna. This may sound selfish, but please help me."

You can assess this prayer for what it is or is not. But for me it was the start of a renewed focus on prayer. In our home, at the very top of the staircase leading to our second level, a Post-it® note has remained in place for nearly four years. On it is one word: PRAY. I needed that reminder. That is why I stuck it there a few days before Donna came home. You might call it my accountability Post-it®.

I list prayer as the first pointer because your loved one needs to know you are praying for her or him. And I believe when you pray, your mind and heart are connected to God, and that is just as important for your heart health as yogurt or broccoli.

Don't pray alone.

Before you call it a night, try getting on your knees with your loved one, at the side of your bed, and share what is on your heart and talk to God about it. I think that is what Jesus had in mind when He shared a very simple prayer when asked by one of His disciples: "Teach us to pray."

From that question, a prayer followed that most of us have recited since we were kids:
>"Our Father which art in heaven,
>Hallowed be thy name ..." (Luke 11:2, KJV).

"*Our Father ...*" Get that? Not, our distant, supreme being.

"*Our Father ...*" Personal. Present. Jesus' daddy.

"Our Father ..." Simple and profound.

And occasionally, try this—one of you ask the other: "What are you thankful for today?"

This idea was not original to me. I read it in *Business Digest,* an online publication we receive at our office and send to many clients daily. On occasion, *Business Digest* includes inspirational tips, and the suggestion above was one of them. I am often amazed at what Donna shares that she is thankful for on a given day.

Will any of this help you get what you want more than anything else—healing and recovery? Unfortunately, it may not. We know that. But somehow, prayer matters. The determination of a Pointer on the hunt is how we need to approach our prayer lives. Honest and continual prayer may not change the outcomes, but it certainly can change the course of the journey and the quality of life.

Pointer 2: Music

The second pointer is music. I am not talking about the best of Elvis or the Beatles. (But I am not going to judge what kind of music matters to you either.)

A few nights ago, I heard a song that I had not heard in years. Some of you may remember the song "Turn! Turn! Turn!" written by Pete Seeger in 1962. The song was later arranged and recorded by the Byrds in the mid-60s. The words are based on Ecclesiastes 3:1-8. I grew up with this song. I loved this song. But I never sensed any biblical basis until years later. Here are some of the lyrics:

"To everything (turn, turn, turn)
There is a season (turn, turn, turn)
And a time to ev'ry purpose, under heaven."[1]

Pull up the lyrics and the song online. I bet they'll speak to you. Especially now.

Music has a way of reaching us in ways that other forms of communication cannot. That is why you will find in Appendix B the lyrics to a few songs that have encouraged Donna and me in our journey. When we hear them, we are inspired to sing along. These are the songs that, for whatever reason, you wake up playing in your head. Many of you know what I am saying.

I don't apologize for giving a plug to *both* the old hymns *and* contemporary Christian music. In the Cincinnati area where we live, several radio stations play the more contemporary music. Ninety percent of the music that I now listen to is this type of music. This was not always the case. My choice of music genres changed a couple of years ago when I heard one of the Christian radio stations offer a 30-day challenge: "Listen to only this station for 30 days, and it will change your life." Bold promise, right? Well, guess what, they were right. I survived without news, financial updates, or talk radio. What a shocker!!

Christian music speaks to your heart and soul. The messages and melodies can help you build stamina to face each new challenge. (Don't forget the Pointer!) I believe God has, day after day, sent me the right song for the right moment. So, I offer you these suggestions:

- Try starting your day at home, in the car, or at work listening to one of your local Christian radio stations.
- See whether your loved one will join you in this step. Talk about the songs you like and pick one song that best reflects your journey. Post the lyrics to this song in a visible place. Let it be your "go to" song.
- When your favorite musician has a concert nearby, plan a date night and attend it. These concerts are alive and inspirational. They can help you stay "forever young" and have fun.

Pointer 3: Humor

The third pointer is humor. Am I kidding? Not a bit. Just like the other pointers, this one was learned. It did not come from a textbook entitled *The Three Steps to Handling Grief and Stress with* Saturday Night Live *Humor.*

This is personal, and I offer the following to put "why humor" into context. I grew up in a home where, for the most part, there was not a lot of joking or kibitzing, poking fun in a friendly way. If there was a joke, it was scripted. The jokes we did have were the same ones, over and over, when people would visit. This did not scar me for life, but when you grow up in a home where things always seemed so serious, you become a serious-minded person as well.

Now there is nothing wrong with being serious-minded or focused, but I married a lady whose upbringing was different. Donna had a father who was fun—and funny. Like a Pointer, he was a bit mischievous. He liked to poke fun and would say, "I don't pick on people that I don't like." So, Donna grew up in a more relaxed atmosphere. Mine was serious and businesslike. God knew what I needed. Over time, my kids caught on and they would deliberately try to poke fun at me and give me a hard time, deservedly, for being so serious.

My dad's mother was just the opposite of my dad. She was lighthearted and fun. She was the one person who would challenge my dad and say, "Robert!," when she perceived he was heading toward the serious corner. Here was a lady who survived breast cancer and had diabetes most of her adult life. She lived to age 97 and was legally blind the last few years, but she would always joke about it. "Larry, I can see you are not smiling!"

When I was a teenager and she would visit us, she would hear me complain about this or that. She would say, "Larry, stop it. If you think you're having a bad day, try missing one." That would keep things in perspective, at least for the moment.

I think my family history formed a backdrop for the stage of my life. When challenges and major stress events began to hit me, I became an excessive worrier. Ultimately, I was diagnosed with an anxiety disorder. My mind and body would immediately go to worst-case outcomes, even before I hit the ball and was out of the batter's box. I now consider this the "serious-mind disorder."

I needed prescription drugs to calm my anxiety, to help me sleep and to cope—even though to the outside world I was advancing in my career at all levels. Only Donna and I knew. My parents may have suspected, but I never shared this, and I asked Donna to keep it from others and our children. There were times when I would privately escape to the use of tobacco, even in my work life. I thought the nicotine would calm me, as I mistakenly thought it did when the pressures were intense during graduate school at the University of Illinois.

I bring up humor as the third pointer because I discovered humor late in life—and perhaps because there are others reading this who struggle with "serious-mind disorder." You know who you are. When everyone else is taking time to watch *America's Funniest Home Videos*, you are preparing for tomorrow's meeting or catching up on stuff in your work inbox.

I know all about the professional pressures you are under. I faced them. Demanding bosses. Plans and sales goals. People who you supervise and lead. Accountability to everyone. House payments and saving for college. You have it all.

But we must take time to laugh, to stop taking ourselves so seriously, even when things are just that—serious. You are facing a serious diagnosis. Cancer is not material for late-night TV talk show humor. But I love what Will Rogers said about humor: "Everything is funny as long as it is happening to someone else."[2]

We all know the benefits of humor and laughter. They make us feel better. They relieve tension. Research even shows that there are medical benefits to humor and laughter.

You may be wondering, *How do I incorporate a fun, light, and humorous tone in my life now, in the middle of a serious illness diagnosis?*

If laughter is not natural for you, here are some actions you can take:

- Buy some good (clean) joke books.
- Sign up to have a "joke of the day" sent to your e-mail account; there are several online sources for this. (See Appendix B for some recommendations.)
- Watch one of Mark Lowry's videos. He is a Christian musician who loves to make fun of himself, and his videos are hilarious.
- Watch current and old episodes of *America's Funniest Home Videos*. They are seriously funny and often strike close to home.

So, while this topic and the situation you're in may not be things to laugh at, I ask you to join me in agreeing with the admonition of Nicolas Chamfort: "The most wasted day of all is that on which we have not laughed."[3]

CHAPTER 4 POINTS TO CONSIDER

Key Points
- What we repeatedly say to ourselves about what is happening around us or in our lives, impacts us.
- Your mental health is a product of what you feed your mind—the things you allow your eyes to see and your ears to hear.

God's Perspective on the Heart
Read these verses from God's Word:

"The heart is deceitful above all things and beyond cure. Who can understand it?" (Jeremiah 17:9).

"Where your treasure is, there your heart will be also" (Matthew 6:21).

What do you think God wants you to know about protecting your heart?

3 Pointers for Developing Healthy Defaults
Defaults that help you focus on staying mind and heart healthy are important during this time of adjustment and transition. Try including the following defaults in your daily life:

Pointer 1: Prayer
Remember:
- Don't overcomplicate prayer. Simply follow the words found in 1 Thessalonians 5:17: "Pray continually."
- Your loved one needs to know you are praying for her or him.
- Get on your knees with your loved one; share what is on your heart and talk to God about it.
- Once in a while, try this—one of you ask the other: "What are you thankful for today?"

Have you ever tried any of the above? If so, what happened?

How does this pointer speak to you now?

Pointer 2: Music
Remember:
   Music has a way of reaching us in ways that other forms of communication cannot. And Christian music can speak to your heart and soul.

Ideas for building your music default:
- Start your day listening to a local Christian radio station.
- See if your loved one will join you. Talk about the songs you like and pick one song that best reflects your journey. Post the lyrics to this song in a visible place.
- When your favorite musician has a concert nearby, plan a "date night" and attend it!

Have you ever tried any of the above? If so, what happened?

How does this pointer speak to you now?

Pointer 3: Humor
Remember:
- It is important to keep things in perspective. Or as Larry's grandmother would say, "Larry, stop it. If you think you're having a bad day, try missing one."
- Challenges and major stress events can lead to "serious-mind

disorder." Humor and laughter can make you feel better, relieve tension, and benefit you physically.

- Action steps for developing your humor default:
    1. Buy some good (clean) joke books.
    2. Sign up to have a "joke of the day" sent to your e-mail account.
    3. Read (or listen to) a Christian comedian, such as musician Mark Lowry.
    4. Watch current and old episodes of *America's Funniest Home Videos*.

Have you ever tried any of the above? If so, what happened?

How does this pointer speak to you now?

5
WRITING YOUR STORY

*"To see things as they are, we must open our eyes.
To see things as better than they are, we must close
our eyes and imagine new possibilities."*[1]
—Gerhard Gschwandtner

Each of us has a unique story.

I'm not referring to campfire jokes. I'm referring to the story of our lives—what makes us, us. What makes us who we are today. The stories may include family vacations or family upheavals, friendships found—and lost, laughter and tears. The good, the bad, and (for some of us) the ugly. From both our past *and* present.

On occasion, an old hymn still pops into my mind. I remember this song first as a young boy. It was sung at the country church near my grandparents' farm home in Jamaica. (Illinois, by the way. Small town in central Illinois. Near Fairmount. Get the picture of *small*?)

The hymn is "Blessed Assurance." The words were written by Frances (Fanny) J. Crosby. It is a song that we sang when hymn books ("hymnals") were still used! The refrain from this hymn is what I would like to share with you:

> "This is my story, this is my song.
> Praising my Savior, all the day long.
> This is my story, this is my song.
> Praising my Savior, all the day long."[2]

Are you kidding me? *All* the day long?

Praising God after what the doctors have just told us?

Praising God when I join my wife at the store to purchase hats to cover her balding head during chemo?

Praising God when I come home and I need to cook because she is too tired to do so?

Praising God when I need to buy the groceries and take the kids to camp or practice?

Yes! Because you still have a story to tell.

Do you know Fanny Crosby's story? She was born in 1820 in Brewster, New York. When she was six weeks old, Crosby caught a cold and developed inflammation in the eyes. Mustard poultices were applied to treat the discharges. Unfortunately, this procedure damaged her optic nerves and blinded her. (Note: Some believe Crosby may have been born blind, but, given her age, the blindness was not noticed by her parents.) Despite her disability, Crosby wrote over 1,000 secular poems and had 4 books of poetry published. She was one of the most prolific hymnists in history, writing over 8,000 (yes, that's *thousand*) hymns and gospel songs.[3]

Hellen Keller had a story too. She was born both deaf and blind.

Did either of these ladies give up? Did they have an impact on the world through their lives, words, songs, and, most importantly, their stories and inspirations?

You bet!! Their stories live on today. And yours can too.

So what does it matter—your story?

It matters to others. It can help others. Not just your past story, but the one you are living out right now.

Telling *My* Story

You may be able to tell that I like all kinds of music, both past and present. Yes, I'm showing my age, but there is another song from the 1970s that I want to share. This one is by Kris Kristofferson, a film actor, hall of fame songwriter, and singer. Most of his music would be classified as country. One of his songs that I really like, "Why Me?," was recently played by a local PBS station. Like "Turn! Turn! Turn!" by the Byrds, this song brought back memories. But when I heard the lyrics in connection to this writing, the impact was different. Some of the words resonated in a new way. Why? Because Mr. Kristofferson is sharing his story through song.

Take in these words. Take them to heart.

Why Me?

Why me, Lord? What have I ever done
to deserve even one of the pleasures I've known?
Tell me, Lord, what did I ever do
that was worth loving you, or the kindness you've shown?

Lord, help me, Jesus, I've wasted it so,
help me, Jesus, I know what I am.
But now that I know that I've needed you so,
help me, Jesus, my soul's in your hands.

Try me, Lord. If you think there's a way
I can try to repay all I've taken from you,
Maybe, Lord, I can show someone else
what I've been through myself, on my way back to you.[4]

Telling *Your* Story

Do you need to be a songwriter to tell or share your story? No. But by whatever means you choose, you are sharing from your heart. You are sharing something personal.

And why are you doing this? For what purpose?

Let's go back over a few words from "Why Me?": "Maybe, Lord, I can show someone else what I've been through myself on my way back to you." Those are the words that resonated with me when I heard this song that I probably had not heard in 30 years. That is why I am writing these words and sharing them with you. And if (or when) you craft and share your story, trust me, *you* will be helping others. When you can share "what I've been through myself," you open the doors to being real and vulnerable, because each of us has lived out (or is living out) a problem, a challenge.

If we say we are not, we are kidding ourselves. As Dr. Norman Vincent Peale said in his book *The Power of Positive Thinking*, "The only people who don't have problems are in a cemetery."[5]

God will place people in your life who need to hear your story. Never stop believing that.

A God Story

Remember the biblical account of Jesus casting out demons from a man who gave his name as Legion?

"Hold on, are we still talking about telling stories?"

Absolutely. Check out Luke 8:26-39. This passage tells about Jesus restoring a man possessed by demons. Jesus asked the man a simple question: "What is your name?" His body may have been possessed by demons, but Jesus knew this man had a name—and a story.

"Legion," he replied, because many demons had gone into him.

"Legion" is a large number. In fact, in Jesus' day, a legion was the primary unit of the Roman army, composed of 3,000 to 6,000 foot soldiers with cavalry! In this case, the name *Legion* represented the fact that a number of demons lived in the man. It just so happened that there was also a large herd of pigs nearby. (Ultimately, poor pigs.)

But guess what? The demons begged Jesus to let them go into the pigs. When Jesus cast the demons into the pigs, the herd rushed down the steep bank into the lake and was drowned. That caused some real excitement! The men who were herding the pigs took off for town. I would have too!

But this is not just a story about Jesus restoring a demon-possessed man by means of some crazy porkers. No, it's about what Jesus tells the man after he has been restored. Jesus said to the former "Mr. Legion," "Return home and tell how much God has done for you."

Luke concludes the story, saying, "So the man went away and told all over town how much Jesus had done for him."

Catch those words again: "[He] told all over town how much Jesus had done for him."

Can you imagine how excited this guy was? I don't think he politely tapped people on the shoulder and meekly said, "Excuse me, sorry to interrupt. I used to be possessed by demons, but now I am not. God did this. Thank you for listening. Have a nice day."

No, he had a story to tell. He may not have stood at Fountain Square in Cincinnati and screamed, but I suspect there were a lot of people who knew about this guy in his possessed life. They knew he had lived in the tombs. They'd probably warned their children to stay away from him. Now the guy was restored. He was clear-minded, and he looked, well … normal. So when he spoke, people listened. And likely, they were amazed. With *what*? What a man named Jesus had done for him—even though Jesus had given him strict instructions to tell how much *God* (His Father) had done. And because God is the power source, Jesus was clearly acting as God in the flesh.

Back to *Your* Story
Even in the middle of what may be, or seem to be, a life-changing event or diagnosis, will you give me permission to be open and blunt?

Your story still matters. It matters more than ever.

Even if it feels as though you have hit your limits—it is not over yet. These are not just my words. They are the title and lyrics of one of Donna's and my favorite songs by for KING & COUNTRY.[6] (See Appendix B for the complete lyrics.)

I believe with all my heart that you have a story to tell. Jesus may not have cast out demons from your being, but He has saved (and is saving) you from something. Maybe, even in this difficult time, you sense that you still look to Him and depend upon Him. Maybe you have been drawn closer to Him, or closer to your loved one. Maybe God is teaching you something now that would not have grabbed your attention if this storm had not hit your life. I don't know. But I believe you know.

Allow me to repeat myself: Your story matters.

"OK, Larry, you've said this before."

Well, here is why I say it again: Writing your story may help *you*.

First you see it, word for word, unfold like clouds parting to reveal the stars and the moon. There is something special here. What you craft may be a challenge. It may bring some tears, some painful memories. It may also cause you to reflect on what is happening now in your life. But I am convinced it will enable you to open your eyes and see that God is not dead in your life. In fact, you will sense and see not only His thumbprint, but the *lines* of His thumbprint unique in your life. It will give you hope and encouragement. As Gerhard Gschwandtner said in his book *Reflections: Images and Insights*: "To see things as they are, we must open our eyes. To see things as better than they are, we must close our eyes and imagine new possibilities."[7]

Secondly (and again!), your story helps others. It helps those you know and those you have not yet met. Catch the last part of that sentence—"those you have not yet met." If you are paying attention, God will place people in your life for the specific purpose of blessing them with your story.

"Who, *me*? A blessing?"

That's correct. You may feel unworthy or unusable, but get ready. God is about to do two things: (1) He will use you and your story to help others, and (2) when He does and you respond, God will use that experience to help *you* feel better. Not proud, but amazed and humbled that God sees you in a way that you don't see yourself. As an old Hindu proverb says: "Help thy brother's boat across the river and lo!, thine own has reached the shore."

It's Not a Story Until You Tell It

If you have not yet crafted your story in a way that would be clear to others, think of it as sitting down and sharing your story with someone face to face, clearly and simply.

Allow these 10 questions to serve as a guide:
1. What is the biggest challenge you have faced in your life?
2. Were you able to meet that challenge? If so, how?
3. What did you learn most from it?
4. Do you believe that at any point God pursued you or tried to get your attention when you were not seeking Him?
5. How in your life has God shown He cares for you and loves you?
6. What gives you the greatest sense of joy?
7. What causes you the most fear?
8. Based upon what is happening in your life now, what is your greatest need?

9. Think of two other people you know (or know of) who are struggling or hurting emotionally. Write down their names.
10. How do you think you could help these individuals (and others) at this time?

Can I offer a suggestion? Get a notebook of some kind (or use an app like Evernote or create a Microsoft® Word document—whichever works best for you). Write down the first of the above questions. Go about your day. Reflect on that one question for several days. At the end of each day, write what has come to your mind. When finished with the first question, move on to the next one.

Good luck. View this as a new adventure.

Have fun.

And be prepared to share!

CHAPTER 5 POINTS TO CONSIDER

Key Points
- Each of us has a unique story.
- Your story matters to others. It can help others. Not just your past story, but the one you are living out right now.

A God Story

Read Luke 8:26-39. Consider what Jesus tells the man after he has been restored: "Return home and tell how much God has done for you" (v. 39a).

What did the former "Mr. Legion" do? (Reread the end of v. 39.)

How do you think he did this?

What might God want you to learn from this story?

Telling *Your* Story
- Even if it feels as though you have hit your limit, your story still matters. It matters more than ever.
- What you share will enable you to open your eyes and see that God is not dead in your life.
- Telling your story helps those you know and those you have not yet met.
- God will place people in your life who need to hear your story.

10 Questions

Allow these 10 questions to serve as a guide for writing your story:

1. What is the biggest challenge you have faced in your life?

2. Were you able to meet that challenge? If so, how?

3. What did you learn most from it?

4. Do you believe that at any point God pursued you or tried to get your attention when you were not seeking Him?

5. How in your life has God shown He cares for you and loves you?

6. What gives you the greatest sense of joy?

7. What causes you the most fear?

8. Based upon what is happening in your life now, what is your greatest need?

9. Think of two other people you know (or know of) who are struggling or hurting emotionally. Write down their names.

10. How do you think you could help these individuals (and others) at this time?

Have you ever tried writing your story? If so, what happened?

How do these ideas speak to you now?

6
THE 6:34 A.M. JUNE 29, 2017 ADD-ON

That is right. It is 6:34 a.m., Thursday, June 29, 2017, a couple of weeks or so before this book is to be printed. That means when I alert Tracy Winters of Winters Publishing and Margie Redford, my editor, of this addition, I likely will hear: "What?!"

The date is more significant than the time, although the time is—well, let's call it "rare." I am generally nocturnal. Since my college days, it seems I do my best studying, writing, and thinking late at night into the early morning.

Early morning for me is a different story. Maybe some of you can identify with this. Maybe some of you, like me, married a chipper "Good morning, Sunshine" spouse. Whenever I hear that, I typically groan. Are you nodding in agreement?

That has been the case with this book. The bell would ring close to 8:00 or 9:00 p.m., and the brain and fingers would follow on the keyboard. Granted, the mind may have been noodling for a day or so, just as it has been before 6:34 a.m. on this day.

As I read and reread every word of this book, I could not escape one nagging thought: *There is something else I want—or need—to say. I am not sure what it is.* No, I did not fall to my knees every day, pleading with God to give me direction or an answer. I just started doing what I have found to be helpful in other situations like this. I let it ride. By that, I mean I have learned to just listen and observe and try to glean insight and direction. It may come from a book I am reading, a song played on the radio, or something said at church. Something that someone shares. Maybe there is a pattern. Maybe there is a message. Maybe there is nothing.

In this case, it was the convergence of four or five different things. Some of them that were positive and uplifting, others that were not.

So, at 6:34 a.m. today, I woke up close to 90 minutes before the alarm clock was set to do its duty. When I awoke and looked at the clock, I thought, *This is crazy.* I closed my eyes, thinking I could go back to sleep. I could not.

I got out of bed, Donna still sleeping cozily, and walked downstairs. Our dog followed me, as she always does. But in this case, she looked at me first as I passed her throw-down bed. Her eyes and expression clearly stated: "Do you know what time it is?"

I stopped, looked down at her, and whispered, "Yeah, I know."

I walked downstairs, heated some cold coffee, and stepped outside onto our back porch. I looked at the bird feeder and our garden. Then

I sat down. It was already a sunny, fresh, beautiful morning. Angel, our dog, sat next to me, as I petted her back and neck. Such a friend!

Then the direction and the message started to converge.

I alluded to this point earlier. Some of you reading this book are not feeling either hopeful or blessed. At this very moment, you may be sad. You may feel like crying. You may *be* crying. Here is why: You have discerned that Donna is thriving, not just surviving. She has been declared by her doctors to be "clear of cancer" for nearly nine months at the time of this writing. June 24, 2017, marked five years since her surgery, the discovery of the brain tumor, and the "six months to live" prognosis from the medical team. You are happy for us, but your story and situation are different. You, or a loved one, are not thriving. In fact, you are wondering if survival is even possible.

You may have just lost a loved one (or fiancée) to suicide or a drug overdose. I know your name. And you know I am speaking to you right now—be it in Cincinnati, Ohio, or Battle Creek, Michigan—because you contacted me a few weeks ago through the Crossroads "Group Connect" system. You asked when our "Staying Resilient When Life Throws You More Than a Curveball" small group will be meeting again. As you explained why you were contacting me, I sat down and the air went out of my lungs because of the pain and loss you shared.

You may be the doctor I visited this week following some outpatient surgery. Upon entering the room, you saw what I was holding in my hand and reading—a proof of the front and back covers of this book. I offered it to you because you were curious. You took time to read it, and we talked about Donna. You sighed and, as you left, you shared that your sister was dying of the same brain tumor diagnosis as Donna's. I saw the pain in your eyes. I promised to give you a copy of my book, and you said, "Thank you." You told me your sister's name, and I promised to pray for her—and you. I regret not taking time right then to pray with you. I will do so when I personally deliver a copy of this book to you.

The final piece of the puzzle came to me when our resiliency group met on the evening of June 28. (Yes, because you are a master detective who carefully notes all facts and figures, you have correctly concluded that today, June 29, is the morning after that meeting!)

There is a very special lady in our group. She has had ongoing medical challenges, but she inspires both her husband and us. She is always positive and affirming. During this particular meeting, she says, "It always could be worse." Her husband reaches over and takes her hand. Tears come to both of their eyes.

I feel led to share some real-life truths, adding to what she has just said. I tell the group about the young person noted earlier and about the doctor whose sister is dying. This prompts a man who is new to our group, a man I met at Crossroads' Man Camp, to open up and share his doubts and fears. All of us take time to encourage him. And here is where the positive part of this 6:34 a.m. process unfolds.

We have created a tradition in this group. It started the very first time we met. One of the members said, "Let's join hands … and offer our hands to pray over _____" (name of person needing support). Subsequently, if a group member decides to share about a personal challenge or physical need, we have repeated this same joining of hands and "praying over" the individual. In one case, a lady for whom we had prayed reported that in the week following our meeting she experienced (for the first time) some medical relief and direction.

Now please, don't think we practice snake handling or stuff that some may call weird. But I and the other members of our group don't apologize in any way for saying we believe in the power of prayer. We believe that God can heal, and if He so chooses, He may use us as His instruments in the process.

I can speak personally about times when I needed spiritual and emotional healing and this group and others helped me. And I believe there was a specific time when someone prayed over Donna, which contributed to where she is today—with an official report from Dr. Richard Curry: "Clear."

So after my Man Camp comrade opens up and shares his need, we share our tradition. We ask if it is okay to pray over him, our arms and hands extended. This is a first for him. He is not sure. We step back and let him decide. He agrees. He is blessed. We are blessed. We hug. He thanks us.

But this is not about us, or him. This is about supporting one another. Who does not need that? This is part of the resiliency process. Resilience is not a formula. It involves people.

As I sat with our group last evening, I asked: "Do you remember the movie *Cast Away* with Tom Hanks playing the role of Chuck Noland?" (There is a funny story about me and Tom Hanks, and some of you reading this will understand. Maybe that will be revealed in my next book! OK, time to add a smiley face!)

Anyway, I then asked: "Who else was on the island with Chuck Noland? Who provided him support, hope, and resiliency?"

Our group members looked at me as though I had two heads and three noses. (If you haven't seen the movie, Noland survives a plane crash, but ends up on an uninhabited island—alone.)

I paused. The group awaited my answer. I said, matter-of-factly, "Wilson."

They got it! Do you? Would Chuck Noland have survived without Wilson, a stray soccer ball that Noland drew a face on, named, and turned into his friend and companion? I do not know. We will never know.

Can you be a Wilson to someone—someone you love or someone you do not know or have not yet met? I believe you can. Do you? You should.

If there is anything you take from this book and me, it is this: Keep fighting. Don't give in or give up. You may feel unworthy. You may feel like a loser. I speak very personally to you here—God did not give up on me, and He will not give up on you. He, amazingly, uses cracked vessels.

Jesus recruited twelve ordinary men who became the twelve apostles, not the top twelve local CEOs. (Please, no offense to CEOs. They are important to organizations. I have worked for several CEOs in my career—good ones!)

Resiliency cannot take place without people, and preferably, a group of like-minded people. People who care. People who are hurting and broken—just like me, just like you. That is why I have included study guides and questions at the end of chapters 1–5. The book can be used as a small-group guide, or individually. In whatever way it is used, I hope it will lead people to share with one another.

But this last chapter is different. There are no questions or fill-ins. That is because I believe the greatest challenge we face is that we allow our circumstances—the curveballs—to mess with our minds. That ultimate challenge can't be dealt with simply by reading questions or Scripture verses, or by filling in blanks. As helpful as those steps are, they lack one thing.

This final chapter takes us back to Pointer 1 in chapter 4. It takes us to where we all need to spend more time. On our knees. Quiet. Eyes closed. Head down. Being honest with God. Being honest with ourselves. Asking God to speak to us. Asking Him for help. Asking Him for something that He, amazingly, already has offered to us because of His Son: forgiveness. It's something we cannot earn and certainly do not deserve. Something that often we find so hard to extend to another "Wilson," who has not only a face, but a heart and soul, and who may be hurting or have been hurt in ways we cannot understand, see, or discern.

I conclude with two Scripture passages that I trust and hope add a punctuation mark and cause you to nod and be refreshed.

> "The LORD is my strength and my shield;
> my heart trusts in him, and he helps me.
> My heart leaps for joy,
> and with my song I praise him."
> (Psalm 28:7)

> "Whom have I in heaven but you?
> And earth has nothing I desire besides you.
> My flesh and my heart may fail,
> but God is the strength of my heart and my portion forever."
> (Psalm 73:25, 26)

CONCLUSION/WRAP-UP

This is a chance to pull things together. To summarize. To step aside and look back, look inside, and look ahead. And to share a few words from Donna.

Why?

We all need to know someone else who *has* walked or *is* walking the same path we are. And we need to have that someone not only observe, but engage us. We can learn from this journey. Regardless of the outcome, we can be better or bitter. We can make a difference or not. We have choices.

Reality.

We are not alone. To use a football analogy, our instinct tells us to try a solo tackle. But reality says we need backup; we need teammates. We need to pray. We need mentors—and we need to mentor. We need to listen to God in song. We need to take time to laugh.

We have hope.

In his reading "Cancer Is So Limited," Robert Lynn voices what cancer (or any other life-threatening disease) cannot do. Included in his list is this simple phrase: "It cannot shatter hope."[1] (See Appendix C for the complete reading.)

Jesus is our hope. He is real. He listens and guides. He sees what we cannot. He has not given up on us, even though we may have given up on Him.

We do not seek pain and suffering, nor do we cope with it well when it is our turn. But we each have a story to tell. Our stories can bring hope and encouragement to others (and to ourselves!) when we share those stories and engage in caring for and about others.

God is not distant.

In college, I took a class in Shakespeare. Really! A line from William Shakespeare's arguably most famous play, *Hamlet*, may resonate with you. In class, we had to break into groups to read the play. During this exercise, I had the line that I (for some reason) remember to this day:

"There's a Divinity that shapes our ends,
Rough-hew them how we will."[2]

Granted, we would never use such words today to describe how God pursues us or shapes our lives, but back then it was a big deal for Hamlet (and therefore, Shakespeare) to make this statement. It describes God as one who intercedes in our lives. He seeks to get our attention—whether we are seeking Him or not, whether we acknowledge Him or not. We are not floating on the ocean of life in a boat without a rudder or sails. We may become lost and paralyzed in a storm, but all is not lost. I heard a good question recently on the Christian radio station noted earlier: "If blessings were like raindrops, how wet would you be?"[3]

We need to take action.

In each chapter of this book, there are assignments and challenges. Regardless of the outcome or what we are going through, personal and spiritual growth comes with work, like anything else in life.

> King David knew this. In Psalm 25:4, 5 he wrote:
> "Show me your ways, LORD,
>   teach me your paths.
> Guide me in your truth and teach me,
>   for you are God my Savior,
>   and my hope is in you all day long."

We can help each other in this process as we reach out to others, both to stretch ourselves *and* strengthen one another.

Reminders for when we talk to and support others.

Donna has shared with me some things we should not say (based upon what others—meaning well—have told her during this journey).

> What *not* to say:
> - "This is God's will."
> - "I don't know why my friend was not able to survive, yet you have."
> - "It could be worse."
> - "All things work for God's good." (This, of course, is a misquote or misapplication from Romans 8:28, which says: "And we know that in all things God works for the good of those who love him, who have been called according to his purpose.")
> - "Do you need help getting your affairs in order?"

What *to* do and say:

- Say very little.
- Listen.
- Very simply ask: "How can I help?" "Can I/we pray with you now?"
- Say: "I will be here next Friday to help prepare a meal and clean, if that is OK."

You get the picture. Love is listening ... learning ... and practical help.

APPENDIX A: DONNA'S STORY

Donna's Story: Rising Above Glioblastoma[1]
April 1, 2016

Brain cancer has not stopped Larry and Donna,
married for nearly 38 years, from cherishing their time together.

As the UC Brain Tumor Center leaps into spring with its annual wine tasting event on April 21, and the opening of online registration for Walk Ahead for a Brain Tumor Cure, one Cincinnati couple is more than ready to join in: Donna Blundred, a four-year survivor of glioblastoma multiforme, and her husband, Larry.

Donna and Larry will attend the winetasting at the Cincinnati Museum Center, where they will toast Donna's perseverance, and they will head up the "Donna's Thrivers" team once again at the seventh annual Walk Ahead on October 23.

Their story is one that offers hope for patients with glioblastoma, the most virulent of brain cancers, but one that scientists at the UC Brain Tumor Center and elsewhere are aggressively studying. Proceeds from the winetasting and Walk Ahead have already helped fund multiple pilot research grants for the cadre of UC cancer researchers who work determinedly to crack glioblastoma's molecular code.

Donna has been treated with the usual array of weapons against glioblastoma: surgery to remove the bulk of the tumor, radiation, and chemotherapy.

In addition, Donna and Larry researched and crafted their own high-powered nutritional program. Under the guidance of their neuro-oncologist, Donna follows a regimen that includes low-fat protein, ample cruciferous vegetables, reduced carbohydrates and sugar, vitamin supplements, fish oil, garlic, flax seed oil, ginseng, turmeric, and baking soda.

A tumor is discovered

Donna's story began in June 2012, when she returned home from a trip to Nashville to visit Larry's and her daughter. Struck by sudden and violent nausea and headache, she bolted for the bathroom. "I was holding my head and thinking, 'Is this what it feels like when you need to call the ambulance?'" Donna recalls.

Larry, who was in Chicago on a business trip, grew concerned when Donna—who had collapsed on the floor—failed to answer his calls or return his texts. He summoned neighbors and son Rob, who rushed over and called 911. As Donna floated in and out of consciousness, an EMT asked whether she could tell him her age. She replied, "That's not a polite question to ask a lady." Recognizing that something was seriously wrong, the EMT arranged for Donna's immediate transport to Good Samaritan Hospital.

MRI scans that night revealed a brain hemorrhage, triggered by a tumor the size of a baseball. Donna underwent surgery at 4:00 a.m. the next day. The diagnosis of Grade IV glioma—or glioblastoma—came several days later. "The tumor may have been removed," one of her doctors said, "but this cancer always comes back."

Larry and the couple's three children were devastated. "Personally, I disguised and buried my pain, fear, and anger," Larry recalls. "But from the get-go, I wanted to set a positive tone that would mirror her faith and fortitude. 'Donna's Thrivers' emerged, with posters plastered all through the house. This is, and has been, our vision."

In 2014, two small tumor spots reappeared. Donna underwent targeted radiation, and she and Larry then made a "quality of life decision" that led them to walk away from additional chemotherapy treatments. Later that year, Donna came under the care of a new doctor, Richard Curry, MD, whom she and Larry met at a Walk Ahead event and who was then working at the UC Brain Tumor Center. Over a period of six months, Donna underwent four rounds of treatment with Lomustine, a chemotherapeutic agent that must be carefully monitored because of potential toxicity. Since that time, Dr. Curry says, the tumor spots have retreated.

Designing a new future

Donna is a decorator with a unique background. As a student at Memphis State (now the University of Memphis), she was the only woman in the senior wood shop class. There, she designed an elegant end table of solid black walnut with self-supporting joints and not a single screw or nail. "She can build anything," Larry says proudly. "She has a power tool set that rivals that of anyone in the carpentry business."

As a result of surgery on the right side of her

brain, Donna has partial hearing loss in her left ear and has some balance issues. "As a result, I now avoid power tools with blades," Donna says with a laugh.

But in the broader scheme of things, she and Larry continue to live fully. Donna drives, exercises regularly, and is donating her time to help BLOC Ministries redecorate and redesign its coffee shop in Price Hill. She and Larry have taken trips—all of which involved hiking—to Canada and Alaska.

"This has been a journey of peaks and valleys, tears, and high fives of joy," Larry says. "The poem 'Cancer Is So Limited' defines Donna's perspective and resolve. It asserts that cancer 'cannot corrode faith' and 'cannot quench the spirit.'"

"We take nothing for granted." Larry adds, "And, we cherish our time and life's priorities with greater clarity than ever before."

— Cindy Starr

APPENDIX B: MUSIC AND HUMOR

Music

As referenced in chapter 4, music and humor can be both inspirational and therapeutic. Music can touch us and resonate in ways that spoken or written word may miss.

A recurring thought in this book serves as an example of how important music can be. I had asked God to give me a title or phrase that would capture the essence of my writing. That's when the song "It's Not Over Yet" (by for KING & COUNTRY) came to mind. The words reflect the truth associated with any outcome linked to a life-threatening cancer or diagnosis. For both the caregiver and the one receiving care, the story is never over. God's character never changes, and, if we allow Him to do so, He will shape and change us for the good along the journey.

Donna and I have our favorites songs—ones that have spoken to us during our journey. With permission, we've included here the lyrics of a couple for you.

It's Not Over Yet
Words and Music by BEN GLOVER, JOEL SMALLBONE,
LUKE SMALLBONE, TEDD T., and KYLE RICTOR

They are inside your head.
You got a voice that says,
"You won't get past this one.
You won't win your freedom."

It's like a constant war,
and you want to settle that score,
but you're bruised and beaten
and you feel defeated.
This goes out to the heaviest heart.

[Chorus]
Oh, to ev'ryone who's hit their limit,
it's not over yet, it's not over yet.
And even when you think you're finished,
it's not over yet, it's not over yet.
Keep on fighting out of the dark,
into the light; it's not over.
Hope is rising; never give in, never give up.
It's not over ye-e-et.

Game, set, match.
It's time to put it in your past.
Feel the winter leaving;
it's redemption season.

Long live the young at heart!
Here's to a brand new start.
We're revived and breathing
to live a life of freedom.

[Bridge]
Life is a race we run,
so run 'til the race is won.
Don't you ever give up,
oh no, never give up.

Thrive

Words and Music by MARK HALL and MATTHEW WEST

Here in this worn and weary land
where many a dream has died,
like a tree planted by the water,
we never will run dry.

So, living water flowing through,
God, we thirst for more of You.
Fill our hearts, and flood our souls
with one desire.

[Chorus]:
Just to know You, and to make You known.
We lift Your name on high.
Shine like the sun; make darkness run and hide.
We know we were made for so much more
than ordinary lives.
It's time for us to more than just survive:
we were made to thrive

Into Your Word we're digging deep
to know our Father's heart.
Into the world, we're reaching out
to show them who You are.

So living water flowing through,
God, we thirst for more of You.
Fill our hearts, and flood our souls
with one desire.

[Bridge]
Joy unspeakable, faith unsinkable,
love unstoppable, anything is possible.

[Ending]
We were made to thrive.

Humor

For many of us, humor and laughter are the fabrics of our lives. Just like Uncle Albert in the musical *Mary Poppins,* we love to laugh. For others, laughter takes a little more work. Listed here are some resources that might help you get started as you make time to incorporate humor in your daily routine.

America's Funniest Home Videos
Go to: www.AFV.com
• Watch video clips, check out the blog entries, or download an app.

Books (check for print and Kindle editions)
• *Live Long and Die Laughing* by Mark Lowry (Word Publishing, 2000).
• *The Treasury of Clean Jokes* by Tal D. Bonham (Broadman & Holman Pub, April 1997). Google search other books by this author.
• Google search "clean jokes books."

Christian comedy
Go to: www.christiancomedyacts.com/comedians.
• Find and enjoy comedians such as John Felts, Tim Hawkins, Chonda Pierce and more!

Mark Lowry, Christian comedian
www.marklowry.com
• Check Mark Lowry's website for concerts and events. See the online store for a list of books, DVDs, and CDs available.

Additional websites
• Sign up for free daily e-mails: www.ajokeaday.com
• Search more than 50 categories of clean jokes: www.jokes.christiansunite.com

APPENDIX C

"Cancer Is So Limited"
by Robert L. Lynn

They've sentenced you with invisible cells that
secret themselves deep in body recesses and multiply
lymphatic assault on vital functions.

Can cancer conquer you?
I doubt it, for the strengths I see in you
have nothing to do with cells and blood and muscle.

For cancer is so limited—
It cannot cripple love.
It cannot shatter hope.
It cannot corrode faith.
It cannot eat away peace.
It cannot destroy confidence.
It cannot kill friendship.
It cannot shut out memories.
It cannot silence courage.
It cannot invade the soul.
It cannot reduce eternal life.
It cannot quench the spirit.
It cannot cancel resurrection.

Can cancer conquer you?
I doubt it, for the strengths I see in you
have nothing to do with cells and blood and muscle.

ENDNOTES

DEDICATION
1. "Yogi Berra Quote," BrainyQuote, accessed April 23, 2017, www.brainyquote.com/quote/quotes/y/yogiberra110034.html.

FOREWORD
1. National Brain Tumor Society, braintumor.org/brain-tumor-information/understanding-brain-tumors/.
2. American Brain Tumor Association report, www.abta.org/about-us/news/brain-tumor-statistics/?print=t. Courtesy of Kathy Nullmeier, Associate Director of Development, The University of Cincinnati Gardner Neuroscience Institute.

PREFACE
1. Covey, Stephen R. *The 7 Habits of Highly Effective People*® (New York: Free Press, 1989, 2004 by Stephen R. Covey), 95.

INTRODUCTION
1. Beechem, Kathy. *So Far, So Good: A Memoir of a Brain Tumor Patient and His Caregiver* (Durham, CT: Strategic Book Group, www.StrategicBookClub.com, 2011 by Kathy Beechem).
2. "Reasons Why God Created Eve;" various sources, origin and author unknown.

CHAPTER 1
1. "Anne Lamott Quotes," Goodreads, accessed April 23, 2017, www.goodreads.com/author/quotes/7113.Anne_Lamott.
2. "Is it Wrong to be Angry With God?," Got Questions Ministries, accessed July 17, 2017, [https://www.gotquestions.org/angry-with-God.html]

CHAPTER 2
1. "John F. Kennedy Quotes," Goodreads, accessed April 23, 2017, www.goodreads.com/author/quotes/3047.John_F_Kennedy.

CHAPTER 3
1. "Helen Keller Quotes," Goodreads, accessed April 23, 2017, www.goodreads.com/author/quotes/7275.Helen_Keller.
2. "Abraham Lincoln Quotes," Goodreads, accessed April 23, 2017, www.goodreads.com/author/quotes/229.Abraham_Lincoln.

CHAPTER 4
1. "TURN! TURN! TURN! (TO EVERYTHING THERE IS A SEASON)." Words from the Book of Ecclesiastes. Adaptation and Music by Pete Seeger. TRO Essex Music Group © Copyright 1962. (Renewed) Melody Trails, Inc., New York, NY. International Copyright Secured Made in U.S.A. All Rights Reserved. Used by permission.
2. "Will Rogers Quote," Goodreads, accessed April 23, 2017, www.goodreads.com/author/quotes/132444.Will_Rogers.
3. "Nicolas Chamfort Quotes," BrainyQuote, accessed April 23, 2017, www.brainyquote.com/quotes/authors/n/nicolas_chamfort.html.

CHAPTER 5
1. Gschwandtner, Gerhard. *Reflections: Images and Insights.* (Personal Selling Power, 2001 by Gerhard Gschwandtner).
2. "Blessed Assurance." Lyrics by Fanny J. Crosby, 1873.
3. "Fanny Crosby," Google search, accessed April 23, 2017, en.wikipedia.org/wiki/Fanny_Crosby.
4. "Why Me?" Words and Music by Kris Kristofferson. (Resaca Music Publishing Co, Copyright © 1972 Resaca Music Publishing Co. All Rights Controlled and Administered by EMI Blackwood Music Inc. All Rights Reserved. International Copyright Secured. Used by Permission.)

5. "Norman Vincent Peale Quotes," AZ Quotes, accessed April 23, 2017, www.azquotes.com/author/11448-Norman_Vincent_Peale.
6. "It's Not Over Yet." Words and Music by Ben Glover, Joel Smallbone, Luke Smallbone, Tedd T., and Kyle Rictor. (Published under license from Capitol CMG, 2014. All rights reserved. Used by permission.)
7. Gschwandtner, Gerhard. *Reflections: Images and Insights.* (Personal Selling Power, 2001 by Gerhard Gschwandtner).

CONCLUSION

1. Lynn, Robert L. "Cancer Is So Limited," *Cancer Is So Limited and Other Poems of Faith.* (CreateSpace, 2013 by Robert L. Lynn), 17. Used by permission.
2. Shakespeare, William. *Hamlet*, Act 5, scene 2.
3. Anfuso, Francis. www.francisanfuso.com/k-love-features-may-2016.

APPENDIX A

1. Starr, Cindy. "Donna's Story: Rising Above Glioblastoma" Original story appeared as a featured hope story at www.ucgardnerneuroscienceinstitute.com. Used by permission.

ABOUT THE AUTHOR

Lawrence (Larry) R. Blundred currently serves as a financial advisor for Kehoe Financial Advisors in Cincinnati, Ohio. Prior to his joining the KFA team, Larry had accomplished careers at two of Cincinnati's leading companies, Skyline Chili and JTM Food Group. Larry holds a bachelor's degree in journalism from the University of Missouri and a master of science degree in advertising and marketing from the University of Illinois–Champaign.

Larry and his wife, Donna, moved from Memphis, Tennessee, to Cincinnati in 1980. Larry and Donna attend Crossroads Church. They are involved in a number of outreach programs of the church, and active in leading several community groups, including a cancer support group and a group entitled "Staying Resilient When Life Throws You More Than a Curveball." Larry has served as a group leader for both a prayer support team and Crossroads' Man Camp Men's Ministry. Larry and Donna have three grown children— Christine, Philip, and Robert.

Besides his involvement with the local church, Larry is committed to giving back to the community. He has served as a board member on the Oak Hills Alumni and Education Foundation and taught classes in marketing and management at Cincinnati Christian University. As a board member, Larry also assists with the business development and marketing for BLOC Ministries, a not-for-profit organization that focuses on restoring individuals and families through education, training and employment, entrepreneurship, and spiritual growth.

Larry thanks those who take the time to read this book and welcomes comments and suggestions. He can be contacted via Facebook or by e-mail: thriverministries@gmail.com.

Be sure to check out the Thriver Ministries website at www.thriverministries.com, where you can order this book and share "Thriver Stories," to encourage and bless others.

Made in the USA
San Bernardino, CA
29 August 2018